£3.75

CONTENTS

Edited by *Jayne Lanigan.* Written and researched by *Tony Lynch.*
Cover photographs supplied by and are copyright, *Leo Mason.*
es 54-59 © *Gareth Watkins.* All remaining inside photographs supplied by and are copyright, *All Sport Photographic.* Layout, design and additional artwork, *Talks Limited.*

Published by
GRANDREAMS LIMITED,
Jadwin House, 205-211, Kentish Town Road, London NW5 2JU.

Printed in Holland.

ISBN 0 86227 481 8

Ever since Channel 4 began televising American Football back in 1982, the game's popularity here has gone from strength to strength.
Millions of British fans thrill to the TV action and thousands now play the game in clubs up and down the country.
It is true to say that the Gridiron Game is one of the USA's most successful exports in years. And one thing is for sure — American Football is here to stay . . .

CHIEFS

ERIC DICKERSON

LOS ANGELES RAMS

Born: September 2, 1960
Birthplace: Sealy, Texas
College: Southern Methodist
Position: Running Back
Height: 6′ 3″

Eric Dickerson of the Los Angeles Rams is one of the best running backs in the game. He's a real crowd-pleaser and his devastating speed, backed by 220lbs of sheer muscle power has injected excitement into many a game.

WILLIAM PERRY

CHICAGO BEARS

Born: December 16, 1962
Birthplace: Aiken, South Carolina
College: Clemson University
Position: Defensive Tackle
Height: 6′ 2″

The rise of William Perry in the 1985-86 season did as much as any other fact to further the cause of American Football in Britain. That was the season when the Chicago Bears won Super Bowl XX against the New England Patriots. Suddenly everyone knew 'The Refrigerator', and his massive 300lb + frame wrapped in that famous No.72 shirt. As a player, Perry lives up to his image — he is a true asset to the Bears' defensive line-up. British fans had the chance to see **'The Fridge'** in action when the Bears met the Dallas Cowboys in an exhibition match at Wembley in August, 1986.
Why is Perry called **'The Fridge'**? Because it's reputed that he can eat the entire contents of a refrigerator at a single sitting!

HISTORY OF AM

Way back in 1823, William Webb Ellis, a pupil at Rugby School in England, was playing in an elementary game of soccer. Suddenly he caught the ball and began to run with it towards the opponents' goal. From this one incident a whole new game evolved—it was christened *Rugby Union,* in honour of the school.

The new game, with its oval-shaped ball, drifted across the Atlantic Ocean to the USA. The first official game of American Football is generally considered to be that between Rutgers College and Princeton College in November, 1869 (result 6-4 to Rutgers).

Gradually, as it grew in popularity among the colleges of the eastern United States, the game underwent several changes.

The first major alteration came in 1880, when Walter Camp, 'the father of American Football' reduced the number of players in a team from 15 to 11. Camp also altered the conventional rugby scrum to a line of scrimmage. In 1882, he introduced the system of *downs*, which then ruled that a team in possession had to gain five yards in three downs (increased to four downs in 1912).

Several other developments followed in tackling and scoring, by far the most important of these was the introduction of the forward pass in 1906, which effectively opened up the game towards the exciting form that we know today.

ICAN FOOTBALL

The Professional Game

Pro Football began in 1921 with the formation of the *National Football League,* the first champions being the Chicago Staleys (later to become the Chicago Bears). By 1926 league membership stood at 22 teams.

The NFL reigned supreme for the next 3½ decades, producing such memorable teams as the Cleveland Browns, the New York Giants and the Green Bay Packers.

The *American Football League* (AFL) was formed in 1960, but was absorbed into the NFL ten years later. The new superleague was then divided into the American and National Conferences (AFC & NFC), which is the way things have remained ever since.

Super Bowl, the annual play-off to determine the champions for the year, was inaugurated in the 1966/67 season.

JIM McMAHON

CHICAGO BEARS

Born: August 21, 1959
Birthplace:
Jersey City, New Jersey
College: Brigham Young
Position: Quarterback
Height: 6′ 1″

They've written hundreds of thousands of words about him. He's a great personality . . . He's controversial . . . He's the 'punk' of American football . . . He's a terrific quarterback . . . He's Jim McMahon, inspiration of the Bears' Super Bowl winning season of '85-'86.

Two thing's are sure — he'll always be talked about. And he'll always be a star.

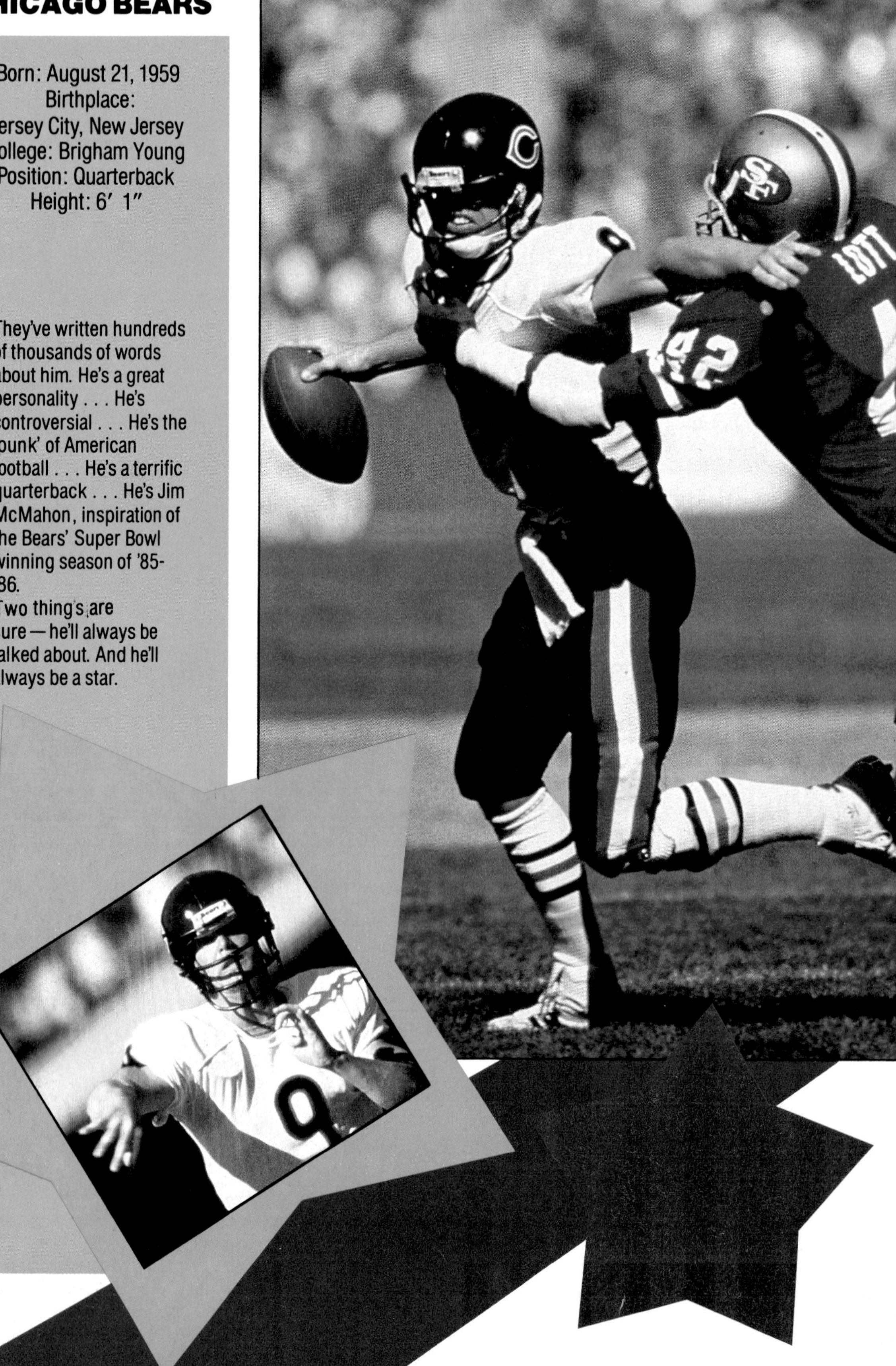

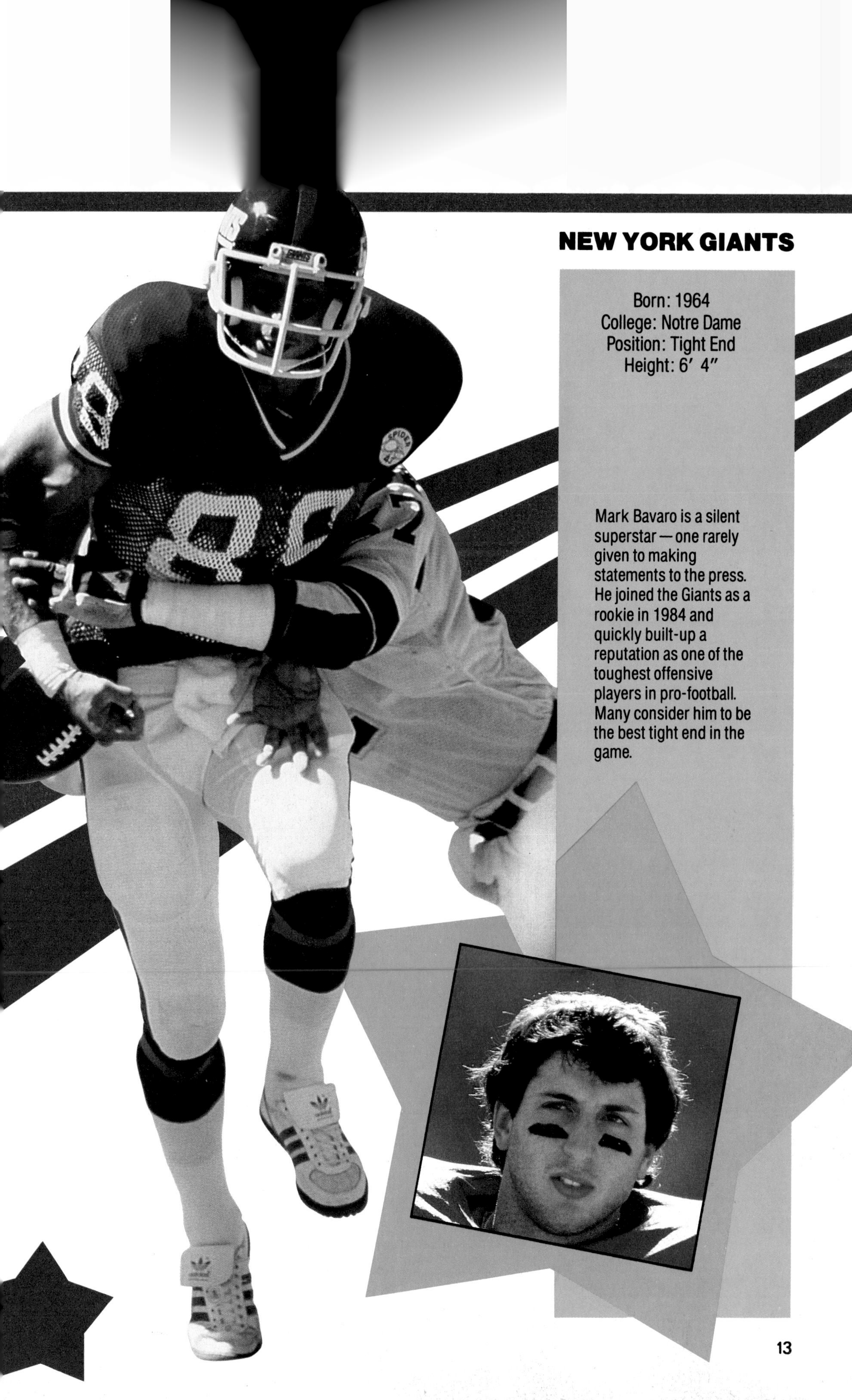

NEW YORK GIANTS

Born: 1964
College: Notre Dame
Position: Tight End
Height: 6′ 4″

Mark Bavaro is a silent superstar — one rarely given to making statements to the press. He joined the Giants as a rookie in 1984 and quickly built-up a reputation as one of the toughest offensive players in pro-football. Many consider him to be the best tight end in the game.

PLAYING THE GAME

The rulebook of American Football is extremely complex and difficult to digest (it contains some 1800 rules and runs to more than 200 pages!). Here is a simplified version, setting out the basics of the Gridiron Game:

Teams *American Football is played between two teams of 11 players. Substitution is permitted (in Pro-Football a team is allowed up to 45 players in a game), but only 11 team players are allowed on the pitch at the same time.*

Game Time *is 60 minutes, divided into 4 quarters of 15 minutes each. However, the clock is stopped often, for a number of reasons, and games sometimes last as long as 2½ hours.*

The Field *of grass or artificial turf is marked out in a gridiron (see diagram).*

The Goals *are 20 feet high, with a cross bar at 10 feet. Width is 18′ 6″.*

The Ball *is oval-shaped, rather like a rugby ball but a little more streamlined. A pro-football is made of well-tanned, pebble grained cowhide. Its length is 11½″. Short axis circumference is between 21¼″-21½″. Long axis circumference is 28″-28½″. Playing pressure must be between 13-15 pounds.*

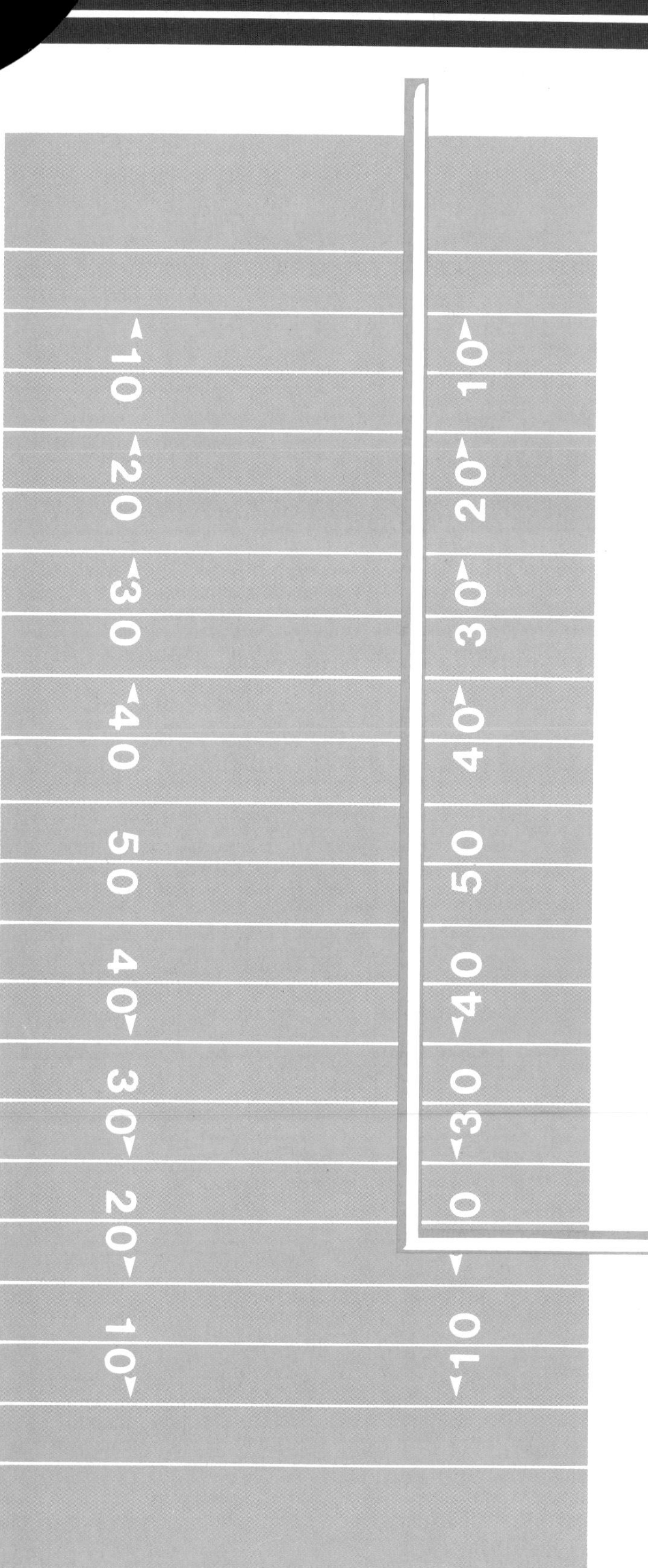

Scoring *occurs in any one of four ways:*

A Touchdown — worth 6 points
A Field Goal — worth 3 points
Point-After-Touchdown (PAT) — worth 1 point
Safety — worth 2 points

A Touchdown is achieved when a player carries the ball over the opposition goal line and into the end-zone; or *by catching a legal pass in the end zone;* or *by recovering an opposition fumble in the end-zone.*

A Field Goal is scored when the ball is kicked over the cross-bar and between the uprights — either from a drop kick or a place kick.

A Point-After-Touchdown is scored by 'converting' the ball (as in rugby) following a touchdown.

Safety is awarded when an offensive player is tackled in his own end-zone; or *when an offensive player is penalized in his own end-zone (a bit like an own goal in soccer).*

The Kickoff *starts the game and is taken from the starting team's 35-yard line. The 10 players of the starting team must be behind the kicker at the time of kick-off. The ball must travel at least ten yards, or be touched by an opposing player, before the kick-off is considered legal.*

A number of elements determine the ebb and flow of a game once it is under way . . .

Audible A change of play called by the quarterback at the *scrimmage.*

Blitz A *rush* by the defense, made with the intention of spoiling a developing play.

Blocking The obstruction of one player by another to prevent him from getting to the ball carrier. Blockers also attempt to make a path for the ball carrier.

Bomb A spectacular long pass.

Clipping An illegal *block* from behind, usually directed below the waist. Punishable by a 15 yard penalty.

Completion A successful catch of a forward pass.

Dead Ball A ball is considered 'dead' after the whistle has blown following an infringement etc.

Delay When the quarterback fails to start a play within 30 seconds of the whistle.

Downs The system by which a team must move the ball 10 yards or more within four attempts. If successful they earn another attempt. If unsuccessful, possession goes automatically to the opposing team.

Drive A team moving forward are on a 'drive'.

Encroachment Contact with an opposing player prior to the *snap.*

Fair Catch The catching of a *punt*—after which the receiver may not run, nor may he be tackled. Leads to a *free kick.*

First Down When a team has gained 10 yards within four *downs.*

Forward Passing Performed mainly by the quarterback. A pass is thrown from behind the line of *scrimmage* and may be caught by any eligible receiver on the offensive team. All defensive players are eligible. An offensive team is allowed only one forward pass after a *scrimmage.*

Free Kick Awarded for a *fair catch.* Also awarded to a team committing a *safety.*

Fumble Loss of possession of the ball. Either accidentally or as the result of a *tackle.*

Hang Time While the ball is in the air following a kick or *punt.*

Hole Path made for the ball carrier by the blockers.

Huddle The grouping of a team before a *scrimmage,* during which they learn the next play.

Incompletion A *forward pass* not caught.

Interception A defender catches a pass made by the opposition.

Kicking Tee A rubber device for propping up the ball at kick-off.

Lateral Pass A sideways or backwards pass.

Lollipop An easily interceptible pass.

Man-to-man The 'marking' of a specific player.

Neutral Zone The area between opposing teams in a *scrimmage.*

Play Action A confusing tactic, intending to deceive the defense. Usually a fake run or pass.

Penalties Awarded for a variety of reasons. Depending on the seriousness of the infringement, penalties are worth one of the following: automatic loss of first down; 5 yards; 5 yards and loss of down; 10 yards; 10 yards and loss of down; 15 yards; 15 yards and possible disqualification.

Pocket Blocking 'wall' to protect the quarterback behind the *scrimmage.*

Punt A kick out of *scrimmage.* Ball is dropped and kicked before it hits the ground.

Receiving The difficult art of catching a *forward pass.*

Rushing Running with the ball — an effective way to gain yardage. The rusher protects the ball by gripping it firmly under one arm, leaving the other arm free to fend off *tackles.*

Sack To *tackle* the quarterback behind the line of *scrimmage* before he releases the ball.

Scrimmage The line up of players at any restart of play, prior to the *snap.* The offensive team must have seven players on the line of scrimmage. Other offensive players must be at least one yard behind the line.

Snap The transfer of the ball from the centre to the quarterback during a *scrimmage.*

Tackle Made by a defensive player, using his body and arms, to halt the progress of an opposing ball carrier.

Time Out Periods of no play, when the clock is stopped.

TONY DORSETT

DALLAS COWBOYS

Born: April 7, 1954
Birthplace: Aliquippa, Pennsylvania
College: Pittsburgh
Position: Running Back
Height: 5′ 11″

Tony Dorsett is a long-established star of the pro-football scene. He's been around, and then some — he played in the Cowboys' Super Bowl winning team in 1978. Ten years on — and he's still going strong!

DAN MARINO

MIAMI DOLPHINS

Born: September 15, 1961
Birthplace: Pittsburgh
College: Pittsburgh
Position: Quarterback
Height: 6′ 3″

Dan Marino is the quarterback **par excellence**, and the pride and joy of the Miami Dolphins. He is renowned for his lightning quick reflexes and the devastating accuracy of his passes.

WHO DOES WHAT

Each squad of 45 players is divided into three separate 'teams'. The Offense, the Defense and the Specials.

THE OFFENSE *The forward moving squad which attempts to move the ball towards the opponents' goal line. Consists of:*

One **Split End** *— a receiver of passes from the quarterback, also a blocker for the ball carrier.*

Two **Tackles** *— the big guys in a team. They block, open 'holes' for the backs, and protect the quarterbacks.*

Two **Guards** *— usually the smallest and most agile of the linemen. They work as blockers.*

One **Centre** *— passes the ball to the quarterback, also blocks after the snap.*

One **Tight End** *— versatile, able to block effectively, receive passes from the quarterback and run with the ball.*

One **Wide Receiver** *or* **Flankerback** *— receives the ball close to the sideline, also blocks.*

One **Quarterback** *— he's in charge. Decides the plays, passes the ball after the snap.*

Two **Running Backs** *— good runners who carry the ball in running plays. They also block for other backs and fake possession of the ball.*

THE DEFENSE *Attempts to halt attacks. Consists of:*

Two **Defensive Ends** *— who attack the quarterback and tackle ball carriers.*

Two **Defensive Tackles** *— big men who attack the block to break down a play.*

Three **Linebackers** *— the second line of defense. They tackle ball carriers who manage to break through, block pass receivers and sometimes 'blitz' the quarterback.*

Two **Cornerbacks** *— fast players who cover wide receivers.*

Two **Safeties** *— the last line of defense. They line up opposite the opposing tight end and split end.*

THE SPECIAL TEAM *Consists of specialist kickers, brought in for kicking situations.*

NUMBERING OF PLAYERS

For easy identification American Footballers wear numbers as follows:

1-19 Quarterbacks, kickers and punters.

20-49 Running backs, cornerbacks and safeties.

50-59 Centres and linebackers.

60-79 Interior and defensive linemen (defensive linemen may also be numbered 90-99).

80-89 Tight ends, split ends and wide receivers.

Each Gridiron Gladiator wears between 14-18 pieces of protective equipment during a game. Modern, lightweight materials give each player a total added weight of approximately 13 pounds to carry around.

Armoury is donned in the following order:

Jockstrap—to protect the groin.

T-shirt—usually cotton.

Socks—elastic banded.

Taping—elastic tape around ankles, knees, wrists and hands. To help prevent strains. Taping varies according to a player's position in the lineup.

Body padding

Hip and Spine Protectors

Shoulder Pads—the heaviest item of a player's armoury and the piece of equipment which makes him look so fierce. Different positions dictate different styles of shoulder pads.

Various other protective devices are used, including thumb/knuckle protectors, shock absorbers, knee-action stabilizers, elbow braces, bicep pads, wrist braces, shinguards.

Hip, Thigh and Knee Pads—worn depending on the player's position.

Rib Protectors—to shield the rib cage.

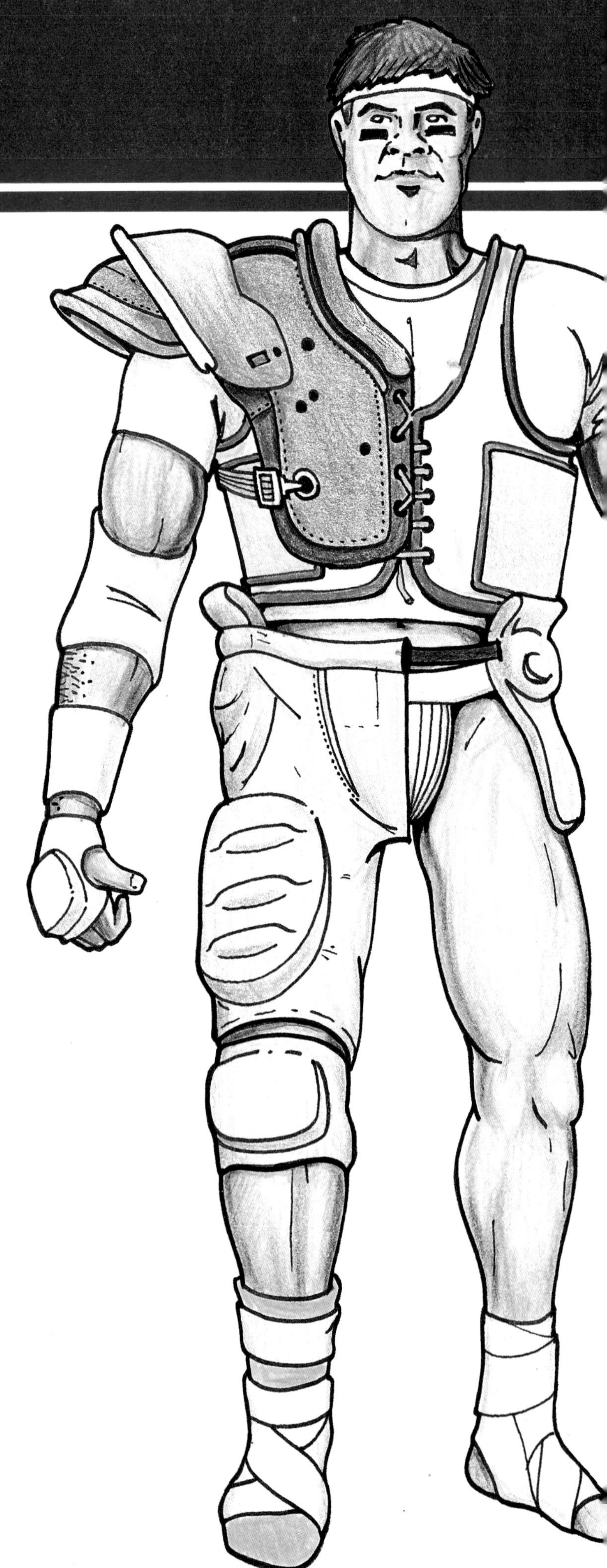

PLAYERS' EQUIPMENT

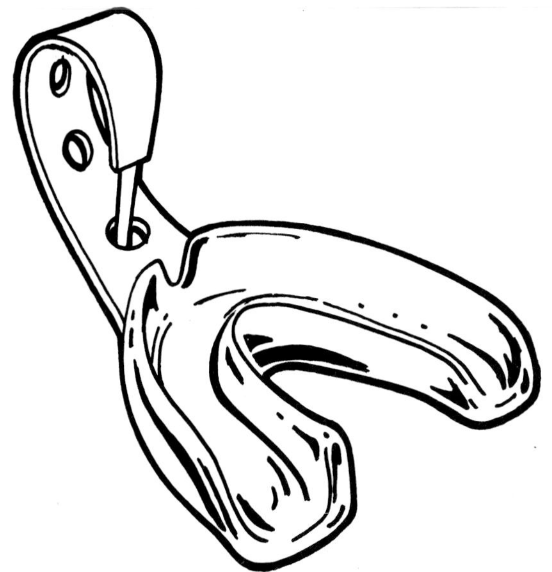

Team Jersey—pulled on over the padding. Jerseys are usually made of nylon and are well ventilated. Running backs may wear a *breakaway* jersey, designed to tear loose in a tackle.

Football Shoes—various types to suit different playing surfaces.

Helmet—the most complicated item in a player's armoury. Helmets weigh around 3 pounds and are made of polycarbonate, alloy, vinyl-foam, styrene and leather. Added protection is carried inside the helmet, usually via special honeycombed pods filled with antifreeze or other compounds to absorb shocks. One model employs an ingenious air-filled inner which is inflated with a pump; pressure is adjusted by means of an air valve.

A player wearing a football helmet is, in effect, carrying a lethal weapon. US models carry a warning to players: 'Do not use this helmet to butt, ram or spear an opposing player. This is a violation of football rules and can cause paralysis or death.'

Helmet Accessories—give further protection to the face. Items include a nose bumper, jaw pads, chinstraps, and face cages.

Mouth Guard—to protect the teeth. Individually made from a wax impression of the player's mouth.

WALTER PAYTON

CHICAGO BEARS

Born: July 25, 1954
Birthplace: Columbia, Mississippi
College: Jackson State
Position: Running Back
Height: 5′ 10″

Walter Payton is among the all-time greats of pro-football. He heads the all-time rushing table, and hopes to achieve a phenomenal 18,000 yards before he retires! Bears' coach Mike Ditka has proclaimed Payton 'the best football player I have ever seen'.

REGGIE WHITE

PHILADELPHIA EAGLES

Born: December 19, 1962
Birthplace: Chattanooga, Tennessee
College: Tennessee
Position: Defensive Tackle
Height: 6′ 5″

A giant in defense and a fearsome prospect for any opponent, Reggie White is known as the 'Minister of Defense'. He is a true gentleman off the field where he is an ordained minister, involved in many fund raising events for charity.

HOW THE SE

ASON WORKS

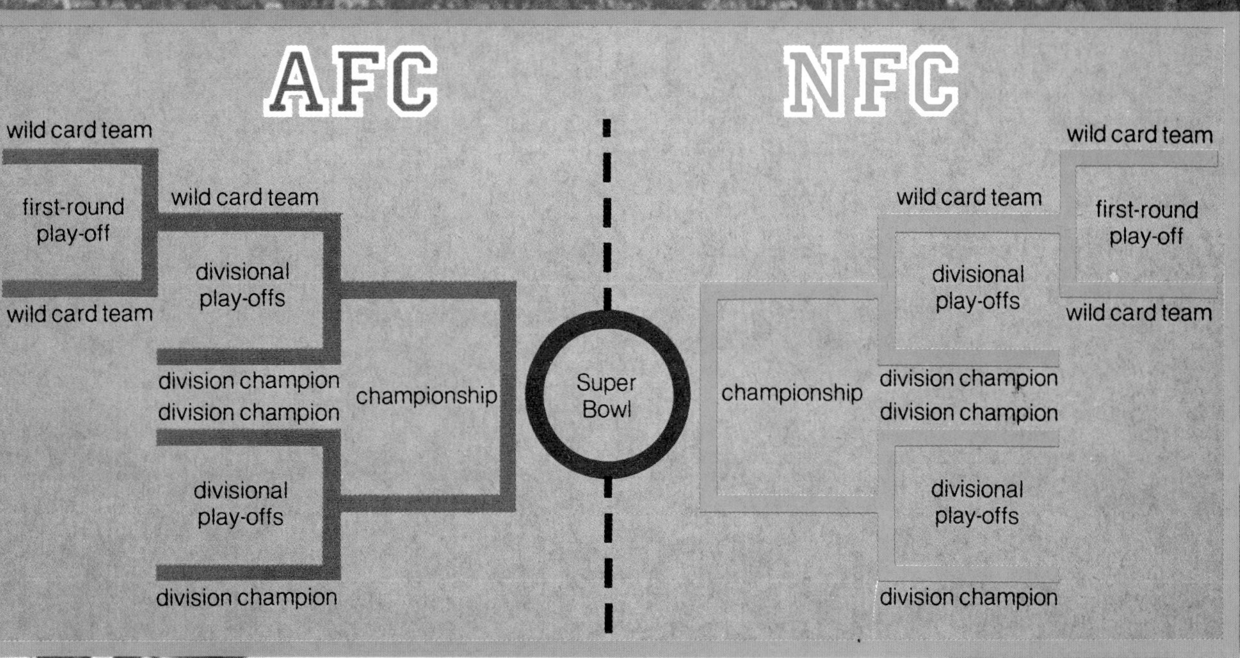

At the front end of the season (September-December), the teams in each division battle it out in a series of 16 games. One home, one away against each team in the same division, the remainder against teams from other divisions. Each team's results are recorded in a win-lose-tie sequence (e.g. 10-4-2=10 wins, 4 losses, 2 ties). The team with the most wins becomes **Divisional Champions**. (A tie-break system comes into operation in the event of more than one team having identical results).

The divisional champions go forward to their respective **Conference Championship**. They are joined by two 'wild card' teams, being those with the 'next best' results sequences.

The five teams from each conference are then involved in separate knock-out contests which decide the two **Conference Champions**.

The American Football Conference Champions meet the National Football Conference Champions in the **Super Bowl** final.

A-Z OF

The current 28 American Pro-Football teams are divided into two distinct sections — the *American Conference* (AFC) and the *National Conference* (NFC).
Each conference is further divided into three separate divisions, as follows:

American Conference West: Denver Broncos
Kansas City Chiefs
Los Angeles Raiders
San Diego Chargers
Seattle Seahawks

American Conference Central: Cincinnati Bengals
Cleveland Browns
Houston Oilers
Pittsburgh Steelers

American Conference East: Buffalo Bills
Indianapolis Colts
Miami Dolphins
New England Patriots
New York Jets

National Conference East: Dallas Cowboys
New York Giants
Philadelphia Eagles
St. Louis Cardinals
Washington Redskins

National Conference Central: Chicago Bears
Detroit Lions
Green Bay Packers
Minnesota Vikings
Tampa Bay Buccaneers

National Conference West: Atlanta Falcons
Los Angeles Rams
New Orleans Saints
San Francisco 49ers

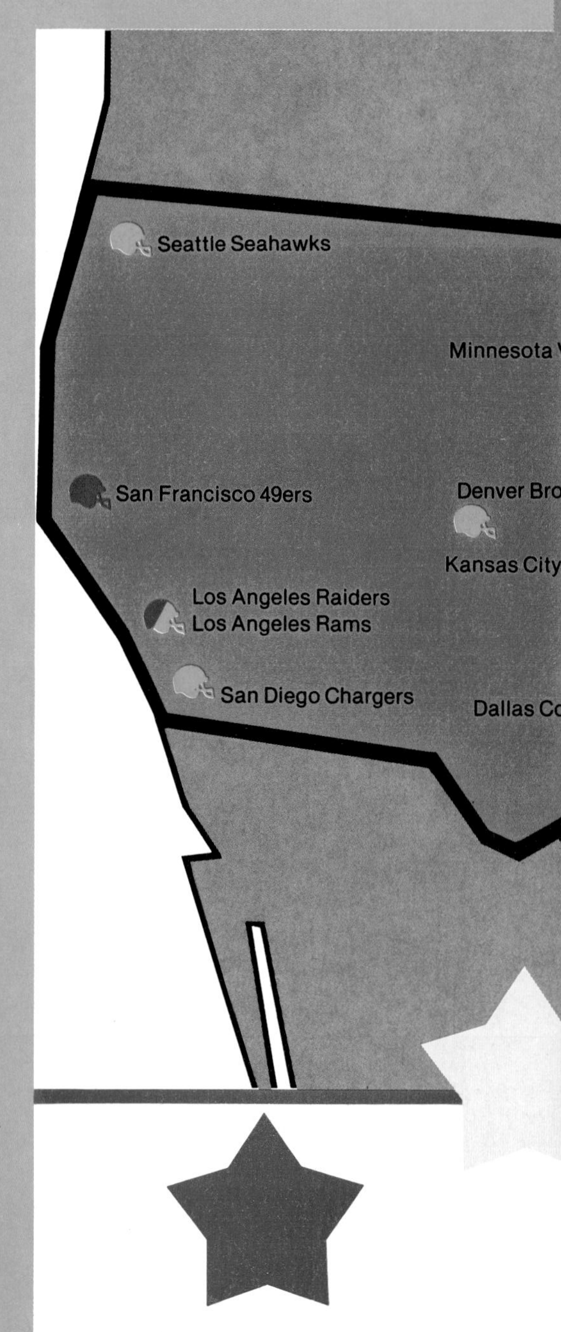

EAMS

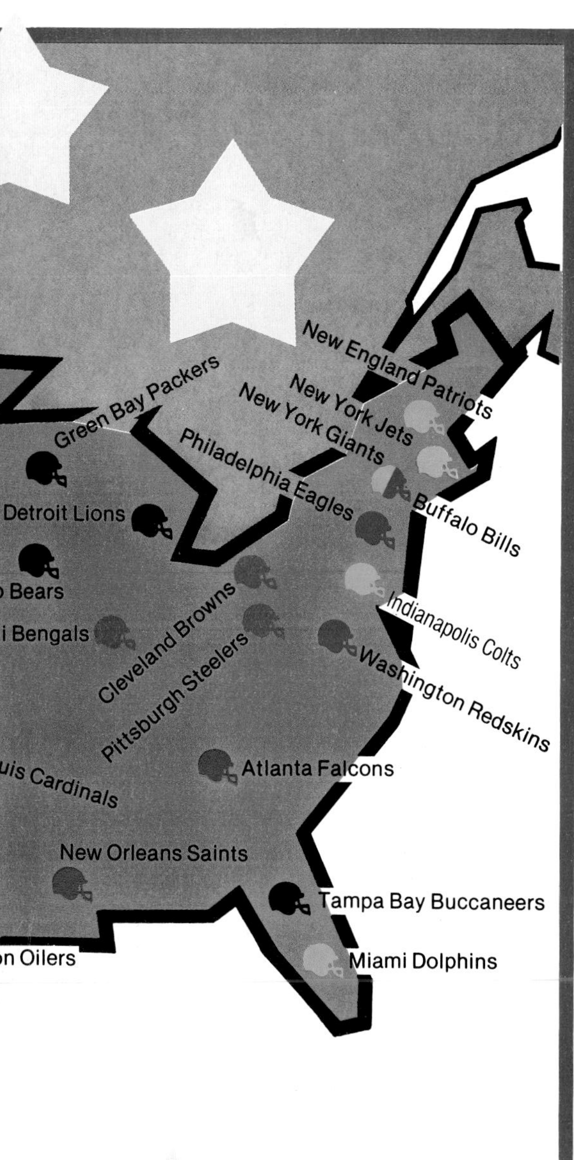

ATLANTA FALCONS
NFC Western Division

Founded: 1966

Stadium: Atlanta-Fulton County Stadium, Atlanta, Georgia (capacity 60,748)

Team Colours: Red, black, white and silver

Super Bowl Honours: —

BUFFALO BILLS
AFC Eastern Division

Founded: 1960

Stadium: Rich Stadium, Buffalo, NY (capacity 80,290)

Team Colours: Scarlet, royal blue and white

Super Bowl Honours: —

CHICAGO BEARS
NFC Central Division

Founded: 1920 (named Bears in 1922)

Stadium: Soldier Field, Chicago, Illinois (capacity 65,793)

Team Colours: Orange, navy blue and white

Super Bowl Honours: Winners 1986 (XX)

CINCINNATI BENGALS
AFC Central Division

Founded: 1968

Stadium: Riverfront Stadium, Cincinnati, Ohio (capacity 59,754)

Team Colours: Black, orange and white

Super Bowl Honours: Runners-up 1982 (XVI)

CLEVELAND BROWNS
AFC Central Division

Founded: 1946

Stadium: Cleveland Stadium, Cleveland, Ohio (capacity 80,385)

Team Colours: Seal brown, orange and white

Super Bowl Honours: —

DALLAS COWBOYS
NFC Eastern Division

Founded: 1960

Stadium: Texas Stadium, Irving, Texas (capacity 63,855)

Team Colours: Royal blue, metallic blue and white

Super Bowl Honours: Winners 1972 (VI), 1978 (XII), Runners-up 1971 (V), 1976 (X), 1979 (XIII)

DENVER BRONCOS
AFC Western Division

Founded: 1960

Stadium: Mile High Stadium, Denver, Colorado (capacity 75,100)

Team Colours: Orange, blue and white

Super Bowl Honours: Runners-up 1978 (XII), 1987 (XXI)

DETROIT LIONS
NFC Central Division

Founded: 1930

Stadium: Pontiac Silverdome, Pontiac, Michigan (capacity 80,638)

Team Colours: Honolulu blue and silver

Super Bowl Honours: —

GREEN BAY PACKERS
NFC Central Division

Founded: 1919

Stadia: Lambeau Field, Green Bay (capacity 56,926) and Milwaukee County Stadium, Milwaukee (capacity 55,976)

Team Colours: Green and gold

Super Bowl Honours: Winners 1967 (I), 1968 (II)

HOUSTON OILERS
AFC Central Division

Founded: 1960

Stadium: Astrodome, Houston, Texas (capacity 50,452)

Team Colours: Scarlet, Columbia blue and white

Super Bowl Honours: —

INDIANAPOLIS COLTS
AFC Eastern Division

Founded: 1947 (as Baltimore Colts)

Stadium: Hoosier Dome, Indianapolis, Indiana (capacity 60,127)

Team Colours: Royal blue, white and silver

Super Bowl Honours: Winners 1971 (V) as Baltimore Colts, Runners-up 1969 (III) as Baltimore Colts

KANSAS CITY CHIEFS
AFC Western Division

Founded: 1960 (as Dallas Texans)

Stadium: Arrowhead Stadium, Kansas City, Missouri (capacity 78,094)

Team Colours: Red and gold

Super Bowl Honours: Winners 1970 (IV), Runners-up 1967 (I)

LOS ANGELES RAIDERS
AFC Western Division

Founded: 1960 (as Oakland Raiders)

Stadium: Los Angeles Memorial Stadium, Los Angeles, California (capacity 92,516)

Team Colours: Silver and black

Super Bowl Honours: Winners 1977 (XI) as Oakland Raiders; 1981 (XV) as Oakland Raiders; 1984 (XVIII), Runners-up 1968 (II) as Oakland Raiders.

LOS ANGELES RAMS
NFC Western Division

Founded: 1937 (as Cleveland Rams)

Stadium: Anaheim Stadium, Anaheim, California (capacity 69,007)

Team Colours: Royal blue, gold and white

Super Bowl Honours: Runners-up 1980 (XIV)

MIAMI DOLPHINS
AFC Eastern Division

Founded: 1966

Stadium: Orange Bowl, Miami, Florida (capacity 75,206)

Team Colours: Aqua blue and orange

Super Bowl Honours: Winners 1973 (VII), 1974 (VIII), Runners-up 1972 (VI), 1983 (XVII), 1985 (XIX)

MINNESOTA VIKINGS
NFC Central Division

Founded: 1961

Stadium: Hubert H. Humphrey Metrodome, Minneapolis, Minnesota (capacity 62,212)

Team Colours: Purple, white and gold

Super Bowl Honours: Runners-up 1970 (IV), 1974 (VIII), 1975 (IX), 1977 (XI)

PHILADELPHIA EAGLES
NFC Eastern Division

Founded: 1933

Stadium: Veterans Stadium, Philadelphia, Pennsylvania (capacity 73,484)

Team Colours: Kelly green, white and silver

Super Bowl Honours: Runners-up 1981 (XV)

PITTSBURGH STEELERS
AFC Central Division

Founded: 1933 (as Pittsburgh Pirates)

Stadium: Three Rivers Stadium, Pittsburgh, Pennsylvania (capacity 59,000)

Team Colours: Black and gold

Super Bowl Honours: Winners 1975 (IX), 1976 (X), 1979 (XIII), 1980 (XIV)

ST. LOUIS CARDINALS
NFC Eastern Division

Founded: 1898 (as Racine Cardinals)

Stadium: Busch Stadium, St. Louis, Missouri (capacity 51,392)

Team Colours: Cardinal red, white and black

Super Bowl Honours: —

SAN DIEGO CHARGERS
AFC Western Division

Founded: 1960

Stadium: Jack Murphy Stadium, San Diego, California (capacity 60,100)

Team Colours: Blue, white and gold

Super Bowl Honours: —

SAN FRANCISCO 49ers
NFC Western Division

Founded: 1946

Stadium: Candlestick Park, San Francisco, California (capacity 61,499)

Team Colours: 49ers gold and scarlet

Super Bowl Honours: Winners 1982 (XVI), 1985 (XIX)

SEATTLE SEAHAWKS
AFC Western Division

Founded: 1976

Stadium: Kingdome, Seattle, Washington (capacity 64,757)

Team Colours: Blue, green and silver

Super Bowl Honours: —

NEW ENGLAND PATRIOTS
AFC Eastern Division

Founded: 1960 (as Boston Pirates)

Stadium: Sullivan Stadium, Foxboro, Massachusetts (capacity 61,000)

Team Colours: Red, white and blue

Super Bowl Honours: Runners-up 1986 (XX)

NEW ORLEANS SAINTS
NFC Western Division

Founded: 1967

Stadium: Louisiana Superdome, New Orleans, Louisiana (capacity 69,723)

Team Colours: Old gold, black and white

Super Bowl Honours: —

NEW YORK GIANTS
NFC Eastern Division

Founded: 1925

Stadium: Giants Stadium, East Rutherford, New Jersey (capacity 76,891) shared with NY Jets

Team Colours: Blue, red and white

Super Bowl Honours: Winners 1987 (XXI)

NEW YORK JETS
AFC Eastern Division

Founded: 1960 (as New York Titans)

Stadium: Giants Stadium, East Rutherford, New Jersey (capacity 76,891) shared with NY Giants

Team Colours: Kelly green and white

Super Bowl Honours: Winners 1969 (III)

TAMPA BAY BUCCANEERS
NFC Central Division

Founded: 1976

Stadium: Tampa Stadium, Tampa, Florida (capacity 74,317)

Team Colours: Florida orange, white and red

Super Bowl Honours: —

WASHINGTON REDSKINS
NFC Eastern Division

Founded: 1932 (as Boston Braves)

Stadium: Robert F. Kennedy Stadium, Washington DC (capacity 55,750)

Team Colours: Burgundy and gold

Super Bowl Honours: Winners 1983 (XVII), Runners-up 1973 (VII), 1984 (XVIII)

JOE MONTANA

SAN FRANCISCO 49ers

Born: June 11, 1956
Birthplace: New Eagle, Pennsylvania
College: Notre Dame
Position: Quarterback
Height: 6′ 2″

Joe Montana consistently finds himself listed among the upper reaches of the performance ratings. He has **twice** been named MVP in Super Bowl finals (XVI and XIX), an honour shared with Terry Bradshaw of the Pittsburgh Steelers and Bart Starr of the Green Bay Packers.

TODD CHRISTENSEN

LOS ANGELES RAIDERS

Born: August 3, 1956
Birthplace: Bellefont, Washington
College: Brigham Young
Position: Tight End
Height: 6′ 3″

A great favourite of the pro-football scene, Todd Christensen has played for the Raiders since 1979. His hands are among the safest in the game — back in '83 he twice caught a hat-trick of touchdown passes.

INSIDE FOOTBALL

Behind each professional team lays a vast organization employing an enormous staff — from players and coaches to programme sellers and hot-dog vendors.

The playing squads consist of the cream of US footballing talent which has been nurtured within the college system that lies at the heart of the game. (College football is played to slightly different rules from the pro-game).

The top college players are drafted into the Conference proper via a system which ensures a future balance in the league by giving the weakest teams first choice of the best college players.

A player in his first season with a pro team is called a 'rookie'.

The pivotal behind-the-scenes figure in an American football team is the Head Coach. He is in overall charge of the playing and coaching staffs — rather like the manager of a British soccer team. Working under him are several specialist coaches — one for each department in the team (offense, defense, Specialist Kickers etc.).

On a match day, the Head Coach is the team's General. He is in constant radio contact with his specialist coaches who watch the game from the grandstand and assess the effectiveness of strategy etc. From information supplied to him, the Head Coach decides and dictates his team's tactics throughout the game.

This page, below: Bill Parcells, Head Coach of the New York Giants. *Bottom:* The players give Bill Parcells a friendly dunking. *Opposite, top:* Mike Dikta, Head Coach of Chicago Bears. *Opposite, bottom:* Dan Reeves, Head Coach of Denver Broncos.

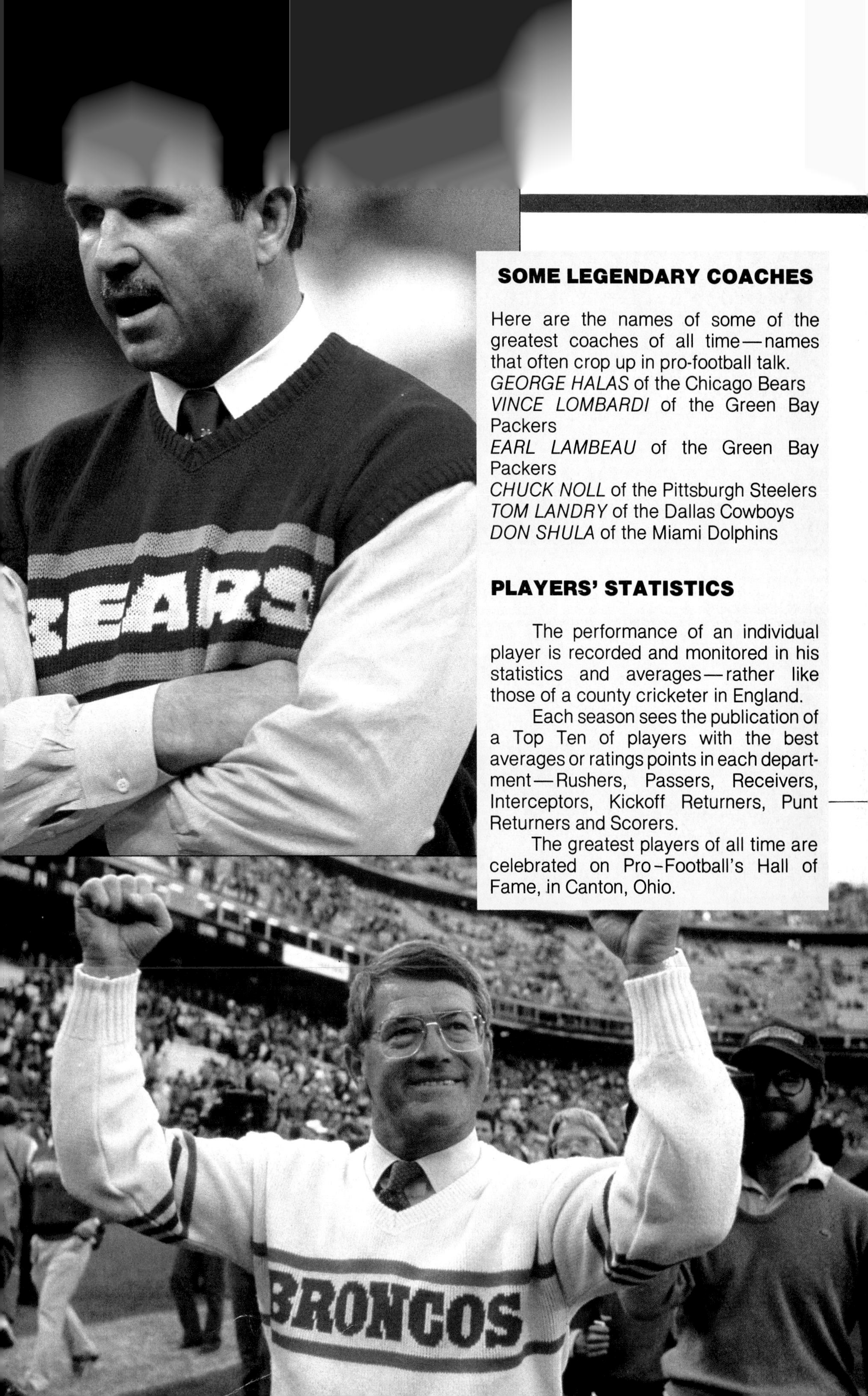

SOME LEGENDARY COACHES

Here are the names of some of the greatest coaches of all time — names that often crop up in pro-football talk.

GEORGE HALAS of the Chicago Bears
VINCE LOMBARDI of the Green Bay Packers
EARL LAMBEAU of the Green Bay Packers
CHUCK NOLL of the Pittsburgh Steelers
TOM LANDRY of the Dallas Cowboys
DON SHULA of the Miami Dolphins

PLAYERS' STATISTICS

The performance of an individual player is recorded and monitored in his statistics and averages — rather like those of a county cricketer in England.

Each season sees the publication of a Top Ten of players with the best averages or ratings points in each department — Rushers, Passers, Receivers, Interceptors, Kickoff Returners, Punt Returners and Scorers.

The greatest players of all time are celebrated on Pro-Football's Hall of Fame, in Canton, Ohio.

GAME OFFICIALS

Each pro-football game is controlled by no less than 7 officials—known as 'Zebras' because of their black and white striped shirts. They are:

The Referee He is in overall charge; signals all fouls, and is the ultimate authority on the rules. He can award penalties and eject players from the game.

The Umpire He rules on players' equipment and watches for false starts at the line of scrimmage.

The Head Linesman Rules on pre-snap infringements in the line of scrimmage, keeps count of the downs.

Line Judge He is the time-keeper, also watches over wide receiver on his side.

Back Judge Operates on the same side as the Line Judge. Observes the tight end and nearest back. Watches for holding or illegal use of hands, pass interference and out-of-bounds.

Field Judge Watches the tight end and nearest back. Rules on blocking violations, holding or illegal use of hands. Also times the 30 sec. intervals between plays as well as the intermission and the pause between periods. Rules on field goals.

Side Judge His duties overlap those of the other officials.

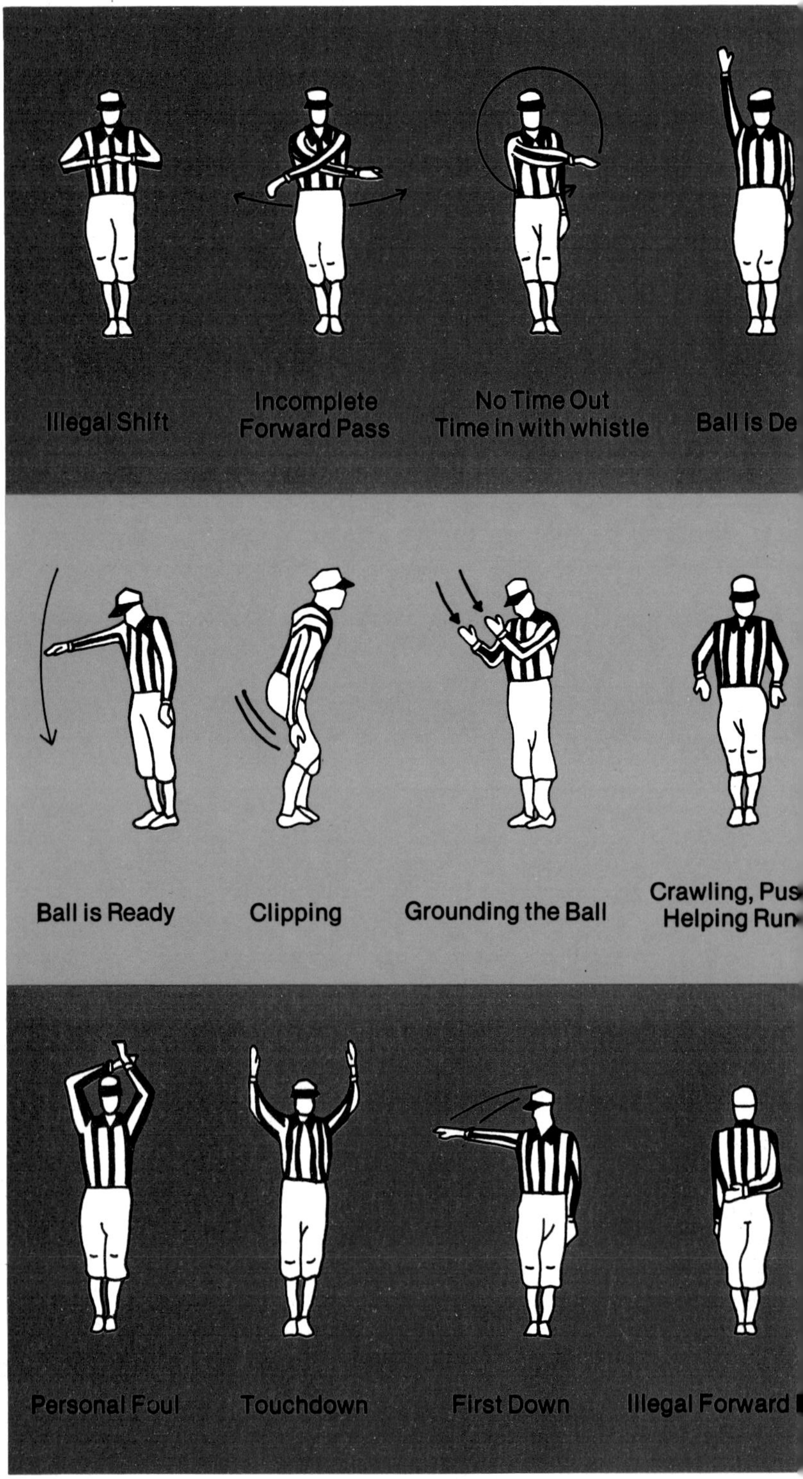

Illegal Shift

Incomplete Forward Pass

No Time Out Time in with whistle

Ball is De

Ball is Ready

Clipping

Grounding the Ball

Crawling, Pus Helping Run

Personal Foul

Touchdown

First Down

Illegal Forward

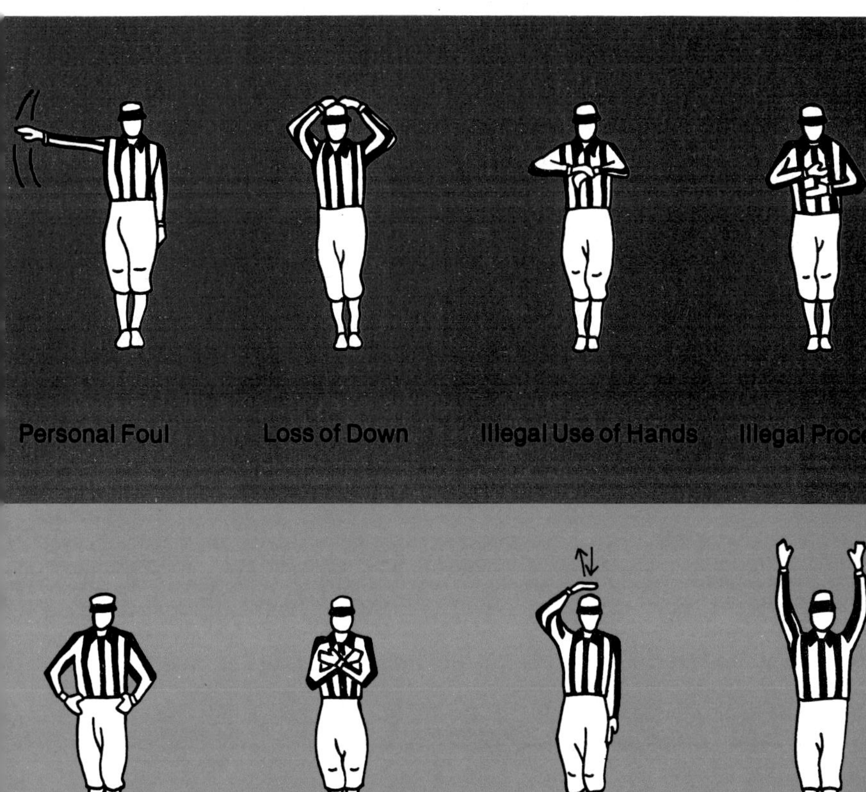

Personal Foul

Loss of Down

Illegal Use of Hands

Illegal Procedure

Unsportsmanlike Conduct

Offside

Delay of Game

Illegal Receiver Downfield

Touchdown

Roughing the Kicker

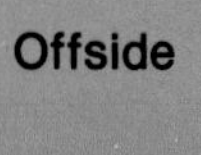

Illegal Motion at Snap

Pass Interference

Time Out

Referee Time Out

Ball Illegally Touched, Batted or Kicked.

MARCUS ALLEN

LOS ANGELES RAIDERS

Born: March 26, 1960
Birthplace: San Diego, California
College: Southern California
Position: Running Back
Height: 6′ 2″

Marcus Allen, in the LA Raiders' No.32 shirt, is a true West Coast hero — they call him 'Rocket Man' out there. He was named Most Valuable Player in Super Bowl XVIII in the Raiders' 38-9 victory over the Washington Redskins. Allen also has the distinction of being the highest scoring non-kicker in the game.

KARL MECKLENBERG

DENVER BRONCOS

Born: September 1, 1960
Birthplace: Edina, Minnesota
College: Minnesota
Position: Inside Linebacker
Height: 6′ 3″

One of the top defensive players in the game, Mecklenberg is known as the 'Snow Goose' because of his pale skin and blond hair. He was in the losing Broncos' team in Super Bowl XXI against the Giants. Karl is a sacking expert second to none.

Super Bowl Sunday is the day that every football fan has been waiting for. It is the highlight of the pro season, when the two surviving superteams battle it out for the world championship and the famous Vincent T. Lombardi Trophy. Super Bowl is also the biggest media event in the US sporting calendar. During the build-up weeks to the big game, endless football orientated shows will have been broadcast on TV and radio, while millions of Super Bowl superlatives will have been written in the nation's sports pages. So forceful is the hype and hysteria, that the inhabitants of the venue city could be forgiven for thinking that their home town has suddenly become the centre of the universe.

Those fans lucky enough to have tickets for the game will enjoy a truly astonishing showpiece, a razzmattazz spectacular that's second to none. Millions of others, gripped by Super Bowl Fever, will watch the game on TV.

ER BOWL

SUPER BO

Super Bowl I Played at the Memorial Stadium, Los Angeles on January 15, 1967—between the Green Bay Packers and The Kansas City Chiefs. The name 'Super Bowl' was dreamed up by the Chiefs' millionaire owner Lamar Hunt, but it wasn't a super result for him as his team went down 35-10 to the Packers. The game was poorly attended; only 63,000 fans turned up at the Memorial Coliseum, 30,000 short of capacity. Most Valuable Player (MVP) Award went to Packers' quarterback Bart Starr.

Super Bowl II Bart Starr was again voted MVP, in the second Super Bowl final—held at the Orange Bowl, Miami on January 14, 1968. This time The Green Bay Packers beat the Oakland Raiders 33-14 in a hard fought game. After the game Packers' coach Vince Lombardi, whose name graces the Super Bowl trophy, announced his retirement from coaching.

The Pro Bowl Each season sees the Pro Bowl match, held for the past seven years in Honolulu, in which a representative AFC team takes on a representative NFC team. For a player, selection for this high honour, ranks second only to a Super Bowl appearance. Since the inception of Pro Bowl in 1971 the NFC has won 10 times, the AFC 6.

Super Bowl III Played at the Orange Bowl, Miami, on January 12, 1969. The New York Jets played the Baltimore Colts. Star player and MVP winner, was Jets' quarterback Joe Namath, who had publicly predicted that an AFL side would beat the NFL team for the first time. Joe was right, the Jets won 16-7.

Super Bowl IV Saw Lamar Hunt's Kansas City Chiefs beat the Minnesota Vikings 23-7. The venue was the Tulane Stadium, New Orleans, on January 11, 1970. MVP was Chiefs' quarterback Len Dawson.

Super Bowl V Held on January 17, 1971 at the Orange Bowl, Miami. The Baltimore Colts took on the Dallas Cowboys and won 16-13. The game had a nail-biting climax in which Jim O'Brien scored the winning points with a now legendary kick. MVP was Cowboys' linebacker Chuck Howley.

Super Bowl VI The Dallas Cowboys were back for another Super Bowl attempt, against the Miami Dolphins—on January 16, 1972, at the Tulane Stadium, New Orleans. This time the Cowboys won 24-3, their quarterback Roger Staubach was named MVP.

Super Bowl VII Played at the Memorial Coliseum, Los Angeles, on January 14, 1973. Now it was the Miami Dolphins' turn for a second consecutive attempt. They beat the Washington Redskins 14-7 to complete a record breaking run of 17 wins in a season. Dolphins' defensive end Jake Scott was named MVP.

Super Bowl VIII Saw the Miami Dolphins in their third consecutive Super Bowl final — against the Minnesota Vikings, at the Rice Stadium, Houston, on January 13, 1974. Final score was 24-7 to the Dolphins, with their running back Larry Csonka named MVP.

Super Bowl IX On January 12, 1975, at the Tulane Stadium, New Orleans. The Pittsburgh Steelers beat the Minnesota Vikings 16-6. MVP was Steelers' running back Franco Harris who set a Super Bowl record by rushing 34 times for 158 yards.

Super Bowl X The Pittsburgh Steelers made it two wins in a row with a score of 21-17, against the Dallas Cowboys. Steelers' wide receiver Lynn Swann scored a spectacular touchdown in the dying minutes of the game: he was named MVP. Played at the Orange Bowl, Miami, on January 18, 1976.

Super Bowl XI Played at the Rose Bowl, Pasedena, on January 9, 1977. The Oakland Raiders took on the Minnesota Vikings who were making their fourth Super Bowl attempt. Unfortunately for the Vikings it was to prove fourth time unlucky. The Raiders won convincingly by 32-14, and their wide receiver Fred Biletnikoff was named MVP.

Super Bowl XII Played on January 15, 1978, at the Superdome, New Orleans. The Dallas Cowboys won their second Super Bowl title by beating the Denver Broncos 27-10. Two Cowboys were named MVP, defensive end Harvey Martin, and defensive tackle Randy White.

Super Bowl XIII Super Bowl No.13 proved unlucky for the Dallas Cowboys. They lost 31-35 to the Pittsburgh Steelers at the Orange Bowl, Miami, on January 21, 1979. Steelers' quarterback Terry Bradshaw was named MVP.

Super Bowl XIV The Pittsburgh Steelers chalked up their fourth Super Bowl win by beating the Los Angeles Rams 31-19. The game was played in Pasedena's Rose Bowl, on January 20, 1980. Terry Bradshaw repeated a piece of history by becoming MVP for the second year in succession.

Super Bowl XV Played on January 25, 1981 at the Superdome, New Orleans. AFC 'wild card' team, the Oakland Raiders beat the Philadelphia Eagles 27-10 and went down in history as the first 'wild card' entry to win the Super Bowl. Raiders quarterback Jim Plunkett was named MVP.

Super Bowl XVI The San Francisco 49ers beat the Cincinnati Bengals 26-21. Both teams were making their first Super Bowl appearance. 49ers' quarterback Joe Montana was named MVP. The game was played on January 24, 1982, at the Pontiac Silverdome.

Super Bowl XVII A 27-17 victory for the Washington Redskins over the Miami Dolphins. Redskins' star player was running back John Riggins who broke the Super Bowl rushing record with 166 yards; he was named MVP. The game was played on January 30, 1983 at the Rose Bowl, Pasedena.

Super Bowl XVIII Played at the Tampa Stadium, Tampa, on January 22, 1984. The Washington Redskins were back again — but found themselves soundly beaten 9-38 by the Los Angeles Raiders whose remarkable running back Marcus Allen was named MVP. He broke the Super Bowl rushing record with a splendid 191 yards.

Super Bowl XIX The San Francisco 49ers won their second Super Bowl trophy by beating the Miami Dolphins 38-16 at the Stanford Stadium, California, on January 20, 1985. Quarterback Joe Montana was named MVP for the second time in his Super Bowl career, a distinction he shares with Bart Starr (Green Bay Packers) and Terry Bradshaw (Pittsburgh Steelers).

Super Bowl XX Held at the Louisiana Superdome on January 26, 1986, the 'year of the 'Fridge''. The Chicago Bears took on the New England Patriots and won by a convincing 46-10 margin. MVP was Bears' defensive end Richard Dent.

SUPER BOWL

Super Bowl XXI

More than 101,000 fans packed the Rose Bowl in Pasedena for the twenty-first Super Bowl final, on January 25, 1987. The game was also seen by millions of TV viewers in more than 40 countries.

NFC champs, the New York Giants, were taking on the Denver Broncos, top dogs of the AFC.

The Giants began as firm favourites, but the first quarter saw the Broncos leading 10-7. By half time this lead had been whittled down to 10-9.

Then came the transformation, as the 3rd and 4th quarters saw a superb recovery by the Giants, highlighted by a marvellous display of pin-point passing by quarterback, Phil Simms. Despite a late comeback by the Broncos in the final quarter, the Giants rout was complete with a final score of 39-20.

Phil Simms was named MVP.

Each winning player in Super Bowl XXI received $30,000, while each losing player had to settle for just $18,000!

Winning Super Bowl players are presented with a Super Bowl ring, the ultimate accolade for a professional footballer.

XI
GIANTS
GIANTS
GIANTS
65

SUPER BOWL

Future Super Bowls

Super Bowl XXII will be played at the Jack Murphy Stadium, San Diego, on January 31, 1988.

Super Bowl XXIII will be played in the Dolphin Stadium, Miami, on January 22, 1989.

Super Bowl XXIV will be played on January 28, 1990, at the Louisiana Superdome, New Orleans.

AFC champions have won 12 Super Bowl finals. NFC champions have won 9 Super Bowl finals.

DENVER BRONCOS ORANGE SUNDAY 1985
Rose Bowl
GIANTS
53
GIANTS
56

LAWRENCE TAYLOR

NEW YORK GIANTS

Born: February 4, 1959
Birthplace: Williamsburg, Virginia
College: North Carolina
Position: Linebacker
Height: 6′ 3″

Lawrence Taylor, known as 'LT', is widely considered the best defensive player in the modern game. His fearless tackling is legendary and he has given nightmares to many a quarterback. Taylor's No.56 shirt was much in evidence during the Giants' Super Bowl XXI victory over the Denver Broncos in 1987.

JOE MORRIS

NEW YORK GIANTS

Born: September 15, 1960
Birthplace: Fort Bragg, North Carolina
College: Syracuse
Position: Running Back
Height: 5′ 7″

Little Joe Morris was a star of Super Bowl XXI against the Denver Broncos—especially during the second half of the game. He's a fitness fanatic who is totally dedicated to the game.

THE CHEERLEADERS

RAH! RAH! RAH! IT'S THE CHEERLEADERS

Every team has its cheerleaders, a squad of glamorous girls armed with batons and pom-poms, and drilled into a highly polished routine designed to encourage team and fans alike. Football wouldn't be football without them!

JOHN ELWAY

DENVER BRONCOS

Born: June 28, 1960
Birthplace: Northridge, California
College: Stanford
Position: Quarterback
Height: 6′ 3″

Quarterback, John Elway joined the Broncos in 1983. Four seasons later he was quarterbacking in the Super Bowl XXI final against the New York Giants. Despite being on the losing side that day, the pundits are predicting greater things for Elway's future. This year, perhaps?

JAY SCHROEDER

WASHINGTON REDSKINS

Born: June 28, 1961
Birthplace: Milwaukee, Wisconsin
College: UCLA
Position: Quarterback
Height: 6′ 4″

Jay Schroeder took over the Redskins' quarterbacking role from the legendary Joe Theismann, when Joe broke a leg in the 85-86 season. Since then Schroeder has established himself as a firm favourite with the Washington fans.

A.F. IN BRITAIN

American football has been played in Britain for a number of years, although for a long time the game was confined mainly to US air bases dotted around the country. Then, in 1982, when Channel 4 started the ball rolling with edited highlights and expert analysis of pro games, the Gridiron Game began to catch on in a really big way.

A pioneering London team, called the London Ravens, began playing games in Hyde Park. In 1983 they took on an American team from the USAF base at Chicksands — in a game played at Stamford Bridge. The Ravens found themselves on the losing end of a 8-0 scoreline — but the event inspired the founding of teams in other British cities.

1984 saw the formation of two British leagues — the British American Football Federation (BAFF) and the American Football League UK (AFLUK) — with teams like the Birmingham Bulls, the Manchester Spartans, the Glasgow Lions, the Crawley Raiders, the Ealing Eagles, the Poole Sharks, the Milton Keynes Bucks, the

Heathrow Jets, the Streatham Olympians and the Northampton Stormbringers. In 1985, a third league was formed — The United Kingdom American Football Association.

The first Summer Bowl — the UK's version of Super Bowl — was held at Villa Park, Birmingham, in August 1985. In a somewhat one-sided final, the London Ravens defeated the Streatham Olympians 45-7.

The autumn of 1985 saw the first international match involving a representative British team which defeated France 7-0.

Eventually BAFF and AFLUK decided on the wisdom of a merger into a brand new organization known as the British American Football League. By now a new force was on the horizon. The US brewing concern 'Budweiser' announced plans to sponsor and administer their own British league.

Today, more than 200 teams are entertaining British fans and each succeeding season sees a distinct improvement in style and performance.

The future for American football in Britain looks extremely bright. Certain pundits are predicting a move towards semi-professionalism within the next few years. And then, who knows? We may yet see an infusion of British talent into the professional arena in the States. We may even see a British team venturing across the Atlantic to take on the best of the Gridiron Giants. What a day that will be!

A.F. IN BRITAIN

1. *Streatham's* Wid ceiver, No. 81, H Daley, stretches ou a catch. **2.** M. Wynn the *London Ra* dives over for a To down in the *Budw* *Bowl* at Crystal Pa in a game they against the *Olymp* **3.** No. 34, Tony Sc of the *Olympians,* plays at Running Ba

session. **4.** No. 37, ning Back of the *kin Giants,* W. ies on the attack nst the *Olympians* at ce. **5.** No. 30, Steve sney, Running Back the *Olympians,* ges the tackle. **6.** A rait of No. 86, Wide eiver, Bradley Martin the *Streatham* npians.

PHIL SIMMS

NEW YORK GIANTS

Born: November 3, 1956
Birthplace: Springfield, Kentucky
College: Morehead State
Position: Quarterback
Height: 6′ 3″

Phil Simms was named Most Valuable Player for his superb quarterbacking display against the Denver Broncos in Super Bowl XXI. His performance was described as 'probably the best Super Bowl game ever by a quarterback'. Simms set new Super Bowl records of 22 Completions from 25 attempts and he threw three touchdown passes.

JERRY RICE

SAN FRANCISCO 49ers

Born: October 13, 1962
Birthplace: Starkville, Mississippi
College: Mississippi Valley State
Position: Wide Receiver
Height: 6′ 2″

Jerry Rice is a terrific receiver who topped the 86-87 statistics. His talents flowered when an unfortunate injury to Joe Montana called for a change of quarterback. The replacement General, Jeff Kemp, developed a pass called the 'Rice Bomb' which became a spectacular match-winning weapon. When Montana returned to the fray, Jerry Rice was well and truly established as a star of the 49ers' line-up.

28